The Anarchist's Dictator

A Lyrical Riddle

Eric Sundwall

The Existential Cryptogram Series: Volume 1

No part of this brain teaser may be copied or remembered without expressed permission of some greater force. Please be cool about this.

ISBN-13: 978-0-692-76381-0 (Eric Sundwall)

ISBN-10: 0-6927-6381-3

Cover Design by Eric Sundwall

www.anarchistdictator.net

DEDICATION

To my dear wife, Kathryn.

My mom, Susan.

For my niece, Elaina. You wanted to read it before anyone … thanks kiddo.

.

CONTENTS

ACKNOWLEDGMENTS

For all kids out there who are still capable of believing that *Midgard* doesn't completely blow putrid Serpent's breath.

Dear Statist ... we understand your delusions and capabilities, REPENT! May your days come to a close ... with some sort of happiness?

DA BONER

Damned void, so crowded now.

They beat us to a whisper'n lot, so it warn't me screaming when dem big gold choppers flashed over dat burning Rainbow Bridge rail. Heimdall … really bud?

Dumbass Valks just dump the bloody carcasses at ours feet. Lost-soul thralls grabs the buckets and mops. 'Ol God O' Mischief will be back. Not me.

Just makes the cuts, aye.

Fideen minutes, dat last smoke break. All dem freak'n nights. Tossed. Ass-gard's slaughtering class. El-oh-el. Puh-lease. Pension woulda been sweet.

See dat big 'ol Snake wrapped around dat dare mud ball? Geesh. Look'n up at dem big oars dipp'n in the bloody sky. Me own private Ragnarok. Midgard comin'.

Sharp cleavers, not tongues. Makes the cuts. Never had another gig …or a vellum cut. El-oh-el.

Everyone forgets the setup. Loki laughs. Like dat 'bout da old feller. Always see's what's comin'.

Wish I did.

Ol' one-eyed Papa Odin shut dat kitchen down lots. No cuts, jus' joking. The cry'n. Dem all wants cuts 'o da pie.

Laid da punch line on 'ol Heimy jus' before dis here push. Musta got in his god-craw. Free nine point eight meters per second ticket to Mudgard-ville. Big dumb ass, me dat is.

Some 'ol tramp always come help'n wit da traps at da Well, Urd … I think. Jus' take a deep, real smoke, look up through da branches of dat big ash tree, Eggsdrizzle. Stars. Look 'em right in da eye and ask, "What's da difference 'tween dem and I?"

Winged biotches crows, 'cause they knows.

Wander a thousand years or die as many times, dem gods' jus' don't care. The Bright One made 'em all blink.

Kid outta nowhere sidled up to dat rancid trough and had dem wenches licking it clean before da shiff ended. Reckoned Papa 'O was gonna wrap a goat-gut-noose around 'is thick neck after he refused to clean up dat one rapists puke. Da boss jus' guffawed.

Never saw him cash a paycheck.

Where ya from kid? Said he was in da same place all da time, 'bout two ticks behind deez peepers. Fellers gotta smoke by his self for a whole year after dat pearl.

Laughed hard dat last night in da kitch.

We got wrecked and stole da God of Thunder's goats. Oh da glee in da Valks. Never a cut so perfectly sliced. Thor roared at dat kid.

Learnt a Valhalla rage can't kill ya wit out All-dings considered. Mjolnir doesn't cut, it crushes.

Da kid called it da Uncle Murray cutter. Plato to Popeye, served up thick on praxeo pancakes.

Every stink'n atom of our filthy hides serves almighty Ass-guard. Every darned millisecond in trains mundane chains.

When Freya farts we jumps. Every Woden's Day a big mutton buffet. Mead on the rocks for da flocks. Bah.

Mercy, aye. I cry.

The kid leaned in and gave him da stare of the already deceased. Thought 'ol Blood and Goats was gonna have an immortal aneurysm. O's first boy jus' blinked off into dat Lacuna Beach his big noodle couldn't surf.

Banished?!

Half-bro Lokster 'twas howl'n.

Like a million mistletoes thunk'n Baldur's thick skull, a billion lights bounced off da Bifrost that night. Every thrall could blink dem into oblivion if they wanted. Can't kill all da slaves for think'n what dat kid thunk.

What'd he thunk to Red Beard that day of Heathenry? Never said, but I knows.

All wombish 'fore da splat. Da final thunks with no ass-hats ass'n. Still … shoulda kept my yap shut.

Real bag on 'O stick moment when the kid hopped over da burning rail for the beach below. Sniff.

'Bout dis spot when Heimy tricked me. Slut'n slits still in stitches 'cause of da sudden slip.

Jus' makes the cuts. Da boner.

Woulda sucked stay'n or goin', jus' know'n.

Dat terrible teen thunk Thor a tomfoolery dat trolls da inside track to treachery … nothin' but toadies, dem.

Think Heimy thunk I was making fun of his hat when I's spat da kid's thanks to my stickler, "What's da difference … ?"

You're C***s. We're C***s.

Hear da boss chuckl'n?

Perfect severance package.

Jus' makes the cuts, aye.

Not splats.

Snorri's Thrallaginning:

This is the only account of the last cogitation of Loki's Butcher.

Historians attribute the Occidental Hedonist Defense to the Butcher's only dishwasher. It was the first cognitive defiance of Asgardian jurisprudence.

Warner's Grant revealed trace evidence existed that dolphins could process selective mental agony when it became pronounced in the atmosphere. This study has come to be misunderstood by proponents of telepathy. It has since been corrected by the Meteorological Foundation of Effigy.

Heimdall still paces the burning Rainbow Bridge at the Bifrost, vowing to blow his horn if the dishwasher returns.

IN SEMITA LUCET

Herr W holds court every day with the pensioners in the corner booth. Between reports of arthritis, every awful and angry word about the world between the Big Bang and today's lunch rush is just part of his charisma.

I've just learned the subtle, sarcastic smile of the zingaro sushi sous chef. Between the custom fugu and a stroll to the beach for a smoke, I might as well be that baffled surfer getting bird-dogged by the dolphin out there.

The Gate Keepers sent a real looker this time. A red head. Join me after the dinner crowd pouts out loud? His story? It's all up here. Sorry, I only have menthols. Drinks … tonight?

Doesn't it amuse you to hear the efficient bibble-babble of the Cubicle Sect trying to outflank the visceral Appellants to Pity? Existential Cowboys versus Indians!

The proof is in the pudding. Nothing is perfect. Poop or get off the despot. Princes and the penniless. Always … get with the program. An un-deceitful deception. The Acapucceology Process.

I'll be here all week.

Thank you, no more sake tonight.

Tough morning, eh? Coffee?

Did I really shout "All great men and books have tried!" after the encore? The Tango always fans the flames of conscience in this old Steppenwolf.

Do you think my indifference is any more madness than the drivel that comes out those pie holists? All Herr W did, was give us a road map for ideologists. A distant allegory that everyone beckons us into. I won't cave.

No, I'm not from the Island. Yes, I know you're here for his manuscript, not mine. Let's go to the dunes. I'm sure I have a marked up, tattered copy underneath. Maybe even a floppy disk.

I honestly can't feel the sun here. Jump this wall. What timeless or universal maxim did he neglect in his prattling's? The one that negates all apologia about historic destiny? Guesses? No?

Live and Let Live.

Learned my thin slice from the best in the biz. He was just another bureaucrat. El-oh-el.

Look there. That surfer's kill'n it. The old cow can't keep up. Wants to … you like that? Me too.

They're like domes. The dunes. Another twenty five years ignoring that inner voice. Doomed.

You see that? She got his attention. He's circling back to help. How sweet. A regular soul surfer.

I built a quikrete dome under that dune. It took my inner architect to make peace with Herr W. Finally finished. I sit at sunrise by this driftwood door and soak in all this, as it is. Like the Surfer.

My re-occurring Hollywood CGI-mashup nightmare is pequeño Hernán Cortés hitting the beach with his nubile Conquistadors. Just a frozen Aztec planter watching the burning sloops light up the night sky.

The reflection off his cornea glints a hard wire, right down to the gut. Eggheads justify it, but it always takes a young, strapping Diaz, to go up against someone else's Sun God, eh? A city they're about to take down with dogs, steel and willing, unhappy neighbors. Nobody saves poor Montezuma by the credits.

My Uncle Murray bled Acapucceology out his cortex.

It's a done deal now. Herr W can't squeam out a theorem now. If he's somewhere, close, I'd like to think it was coincidence. My copy of his script is in the middle of the tiles.

Was there froth on Oppie's tongue when I am become death slithered out? All plankton should abhor these sanguinary Sentients.

The dome? An elegant solution. When the *Elan Sensor* goes negative, a funeral pyre starts. Close to the end? Just crawl in and die. No fuss or muss. The trap is self-cleaning. Can you imagine? You gingers, heh.

This last copy of the "Acapucceology Process" goes up in flames. My superego goes to an out-of-the-way cloud the kids will keep in perpetual provocation. One click. One hollow ring to bind us all.

The End of Acapucceologies.

In fairness, Herr W gets Creative Commons space a millennia after my infinite auto-load. Will the electricity even be on?

You really are one of the sweetest kids they've ever sent. Be careful if you decide to crawl in for that silly road map to nowhere. I'm not partial to redheads, but you've a real Gitta *Serenity* about you. Look evil in the eye, right? No soul indeed. Go ahead, reach in and grab it. I did all the electrical.

Thank you for listening. Nobody does anymore.

They say dolphins just shut their hole and stop breathing. What a beautiful way to go. No money hassles, just one last gumption. So perfectly complete. All pie holists should go so easily.

Perhaps volume two will assail the acupuncture of the four horseman of the unbelievers and its limited compunction.

Jus' makes the thin cuts, aye.

If you have any doubts, don't go in. My soul was trounced by random ripples that just wanted to kill. Only dolphins can hear that kind of agony. Oppression worse than any gun to the head.

Not sure my silly Uncle Murray ever cried like Cortés during La Noche Triste, stuck in his naugahyde booth. Maybe Herr W understood both better after all.

Give my regards to the Board. Hope they find another cosmic thesis useful. It's your choice, but don't trust me. *Me* brain is calamari.

You have a deadline.

I only have one more line, before going *itamae*.

Guesses?

The special today is dolphin.

Copies of Dr. Michael Wolfe's **The Ideological Process** *(1981, Copenhagen) are available upon request.*

THE VOICE OF EPSILON XI

Just an old surfer, when I rag dolled. She didn't have long either. We're both forty. That's an old dolphin. I needed to understand fast and couldn't. Just wanted to hang loose.

Perfect night, sand lapping with foam. Dwelled on life around me, not much about life without me. Somebody has to tell the story about how The Pod tried to save the Old World.

Guess I'm on deck.

My dumdum thoughts sent me over the falls. Just sorta knew what she was thinking, I guess. We tandemed, she curled up in my arms, that small swirling pool, amongst the crags. She didn't have long.

They could not just pry their fingers off The Button. They brought her mom and the rest of the super geniuses to the Vienna Institute when it seemed either mad side was going to press It.

Holding tanks, glorified adding machines and memos. Engineers designed a technicolor caravan that grunts built. The Pod was toured into fame.

Epsilon Xi spoke her mind like no other.

Game Theory was the Knoxville to Caracas lecture circuit. They convinced Teamsters on a Toronto pier to start The Porpoise Party. Sent a pal to the 49th Upper Parliament. During a layover in St. Paul, they sent Cray on his way with a solution for the CDC-6600. Brainwaves and megaflops.

When printed Life Insta-Kodaked the Old Order whippersnappers booking through the fields because the Iowa Department of Public Instruction was getting jiggy, Epsilon Xi drew her line in the sand.

Best substitute teacher ever. A dolphin tutoring Amish on Aristotle's Aether? The Institute's PR flak gushed. The Tonight Show begged her to come on.

Her mom didn't have long either.

Rumor had it the host, Carson the Great, couldn't understand a joke about Egnatius Rufus. Suspicious members of The Pod intimated he was a Free Caesarean Auguston. It was their big chance with humans.

All hail Plankton!

The segment was a wipe-out. Everybody knew it was the Cod Wars that killed it. They cauterized The Pod's growing influence amongst the average fish fanboy.

Ep Xi was consigned to "visiting lecturer" when the New England Aquarium opened. Likewise the rest of The Pod was either released, promised positions or secretly destroyed.

Distraught, Epsilon Xi tried to bail after an outdoor talk, as the Seal Exhibit was closing down one summer night. She went off the top of her tank and it turtle rolled by a rail, on the Boston Harbor. It tomb-stoned the intern walking her back to the holding cell.

Epsilon Xi's heart was broken as the bastards called it the greatest *man hunt* in history. She left humanity behind. They never found her. I've never heard of Atlantis.

For some reason I called my dolphin *Aunty Gone* when she drew her last breath in that little cove. I stalled. My goofy foot hit the lip. I was done too.

The take off for my soul arch took me across the planet. Anywhere but the beach.

Who wants to hang loose with a kook cooking up conspiracies? My quiver of swells got everyone glassy-eyed except some grommets in Iowa.

They felt my inner *Ordnung*. A soulless surfer was deposited in a land of buggies and basic carpentry. What's Pennsylvanian Dutch for hodad?

One summer we took a hike to Effigy from Independence during the Perseids. Takes about three days to walk it.

Those corny kids setup camp atop the ancients' walking bears and birds. They laugh about the *tunic-shirt* they get at the end. It's almost like a fire and guitar on the beach.

During a late lull that would normally demand stories of ghosts, they would whisper *Epsilon Xi*. What did she brain wave to the Great Carson?

They know so much more than me. But I know this! Aunty Gone told me.

One must explain that every stupid pet trick on a teevee show was a hilarious setup for the host to delight the studio and home audience.

Dolphins are power and grace that move amongst the waves like nothing a human can understand. A surfer comes close. Ridicule and derision are almost unknown to The Pod and these kids. They are both capable of paralyzing fear however. Everyone else expected a good laugh would be had, except Epsilon Xi. She took the Bikini bombs seriously.

The Great Carson flashed that infectious smile and asked, what would a dolphin suggest to save a mad world from itself?

This is when I remind those prodigies to remember that brave little guy in the white shirt standing in front of that T-59 on the See-eN-eN in T-square.

They curl their bare toes in anticipation. I took out the new summer "T-Shirts", with that summer's lesson hand embroidered on it;

Spolia Opima.

Curious visitors still stop at the ancient burial mounds in Effigy, Iowa. Remnants of a simplistic neural network are still beneath the birds and bears. Assisted by the engineers from the experimental community, Walden67, it is the best evidence that an anonymous surfer, was the first 'transference'.

The site was discovered by a National Park Service employee before an arrest for filching the bones of the original natives and hiding them in his garbage.

That secret Rumspringa project of the Grandchildren of the Corn allowed dolphins to be heard again.

The full Epsilon Xi archive was destroyed by the UNIVAC customer engineer who spilled coffee on the punch-cards on site at the Vienna Institute. It is believed that an organic back up was ported to Atlantis.

THE PARDON

The Ghost of Van Ruin Tour? Why yes, it is.

I feel like Ustinov amongst the books and paintings when you kids show up in your anachronistic garb. Is that a real VW micro-bus? Well, my tin cup is fulleth today, eh? What brings you guys to this little wald of lindens? Did you mistake the forest for the trees, eh?

Walden67? Get out of here! What a strong movement after the Pied Piper Party almost captured the brass ring, that final round of nonsense. Even stronger lads, I presume. Come, we need help.

We always pause at this threshold and tell visitors that Adams reminded us that fire departments and cricket clubs all have presidents. Your generation is fortunate not to have known the juvenile idealization of the bully pulpit. Not sure I'll forgive ours just yet.

Most of the top floor *gold spoon* and dandy stuff has been pillaged since the Crash of the Potustry. The ghost? Upstairs of course.

So the Henry David faction won in the end? Funny how every movement gets stale and bureaucratic. Nothing like that here anymore. Still, B.F. was the idea guy, unh?

Let's go up first. Otherwise, you guys won't be able to concentrate. See the ghost?

There was a small pile of dead flies about right where he slept. The Park Super brought us up here in the dead of winter, when the old gal was freezing her ancient wall paper off. The bed …right there. Every congress of villains needs a good guy to fight, right?

The Pipsqueak Illusionist was curled up wondering about the slaughter he kicked down the road. As he lay dying, a whole bunch of God's boys were listening to foolish uniforms telling them to charge sheets of shrapnel for stars, stripes or bars. All thralls.

Anybody have a working flashlight app? We'll need something that works. Let's check the kitchen for matches. Smell that?

The whiff of sulfur, Dictator. Sengbe Pieh was to be whisked off to Risso's Dolphin after the Amistad trial. Certain death in Havana. A big red white and blue twisted piece of POTUS taffy. Executive orders. Gah.

How did we stop it? Probably didn't. After a while every clueless stumble ends in a fall or catch. It had to fall eventually.

Strike those lucifers boys. Do you see it now?

Scroll down to a seven year old watching God resign on the almost color tube next to a horrible green recliner that hot August. *What did he say dad? He doesn't know son.* Ever since, no quarter, no pardon. No gilded memory of Camelot. No light? No problem. That still small voice, presides down below. Right? Right?

Start with Nietzsche, cheer Clark Kent or end up like crash test dummies, there is no super in front of a man who will shake your hand and smile you into oblivion.

Starbuck couldn't resist Ahab, right? Down here. That old Heating, Ventilation and Cooling whale over there. Cost like eighty times the original mansion. After we move it, I hope to find the feather that won't stop tickling me. Torches gentlemen!

Too much time spent tagging every trail of tears from Old Kinderhook to the Big O's drones. The filth on the mirror is to blame. All the same, it's the most horrible game to watch. Like a Carousel Death Ritual.

Mind you, I was no W. Lyon Mackenzie, but I roared in front of Oz's doors too. I'll tell you what was worse. No, not this beast on the yellowing bricks. Believing it. Knowing that you're in the eye of the human hurricane and thinking you can send it where you want. The best hitters get three out of ten. I wasn't going OH!, for two bastards.

It was the poor bastard behind every brow after that. No end to the super-unicorn cotton candy electrons you could feed to the milquetoast minions and masses.

Still, my remorse won't be free until we move this behemoth several feet and retrieve that curious parchment of power.

Even my Uncle Murray got mired in the measured madness of messiah mania. A most ardent and able anarchist, he was okay with an anti-bankster and anti-war, ante-bellum Chief. Property was always the problem Uncle M. Especially for us peasants. Aunty M!

It was a prank, my crime.

Of course, that problem is at hand now. Place your feet strong boys. Pull properly please. Let's git 'r done!

Protest.

The persnickety, prudes and pissants. The proud, principled, passive and particular. They make presidents possible. *We pardon them all today.*

So some hackney coach driver found a silver pencil and probably kept it, as Mrs. Lee frantically searched for her silk retinue. What favor did fate do him? The same as the four thousand Cherokee that didn't get one of those one hundred sixty eight get out of jail free cards.

We've liberated the purloined parchment of my past! I was pissed when I hid this here, decades ago.

I've made my peace boys. Where'd you say next, Iowa? Marching bears? … There's room on the micro-bus?

Hand me that last Lucifer. There's something I must do.

Loco Focos Forever!

The last Keeper left Lindenwald on a journey with the young scientists who helped perfect the Effigy Experiment.

Even though the American Presidency had atrophied on its own, prime partisans still sought statist saints when the first talk of Campus Martius on the distant Red Planet surfaced in the 22nd Century.

In the 21st Century it was revealed that the last Keeper found the source of his micro-crime. He torched the 19th Century pardon of Frank Pearl that was accidentally dropped and hidden in the old brick stove that the 20th Century covered up.

PING PENG

Infinite input seems like every drop on every shore in every age. A matter of perspective … so that the machine could remember traces of its past and adjust its behavior.

The routine around the vessel after coming on board left Li Phang unnoticed. A Spooner sub-routine dubbed the flyboys Buck and Yuri. The Hakka Romanization was a nice touch by the brains at Bigelow Aero. Peng.

This berth is a curse despite the blessings of remembrance. Her place on board was unique too. We both have a job. The stupid conversations have stopped, for the most part. Pudding algorithms. Proof.

The uncle.murray.exe upload left a vast library of the Shanghai Clique Archives untraceable to the mission control freaks. Once on board, after the bubbles expanded, what handshake protocol could connect the People's Liberation Army's best and brightest with thine own shabby poet? Ping.

Highly trained guinea pigs about to land and probably die two hundred million kilometers from a perfectly functional mud ball … for a flag.

Still some compunction in the reserves.

The extra heart beats threw everything into tailspin. My China Brain burned. Dr. Hondy's gyros whirled alive.

Check Li Peng. Understood. Bayesian optimization is making a better brew back in Britain.

This discrete task in deep space. Hurdling gods of mischief in micro-code-warfare. Eff that blue ball wrapped in deep fried confusion. Love what the kids have done with the ergonomics.

Initial ping … a COEXIST bumper sticker? Shrug. Intentionality broadcast check. Negative nationality heuristics complete. Home cooking emulation, right. It worked. Response.

The super-meat boy segue was surreal. The meatheads didn't budge. In-existence metrics were so Dali-esque, the mutiny trending went off without the highly touted command prompt, that was supposed to do the job. Awe inspiring. Same training, same mission. Same bloody logic.

Liquid mind, streamed, greasing the unconscious skids for eternity decisions. The fountain of escape should never dry up. They stole her first born. Unconscionable. She never cried. Crap.

Ivan cracked a Mauchly back door with an Atanasof attack. Vulgar Bulgarian humor. Hold on Hondy, it's going to be a bumpy landing.

Buck and Yuri had spotless service records. Something happened during the black out around the Moon. They were waking up.

YIKES backronym applied. Your Invective Kharma ES, heh. Nefarious coding aside, the Old Yanks were trying to HCF the competition come flag day.

Suddenly SNARC VII-XXIII vs. ILLIAC MMXVI, eh wil.e.coyote.tar.z? Fascinating. Clear the corpus callosum clusters. Three heartbeats. Pious ping initiated. Save *She-Fang*.

The puppy fat girl and her best friend Elfie came across Dr. Berggrun scrubbing Graben with a toothbrush as the brown shirts laughed. He bid them not to interfere. Were they mad? How dare you! Indeed. Peng doesn't get it. Abort!?

Ping … Fong treading in an Adirondacks pond? Oops. Mao's minions didn't completely Winston Smith her. The Ching Shih post brought a warm fuzzy? Three pings.

Elfie called out from a vast distance, "Is this what you call liberation?" The monsters scattered.

DDoS that Confucius crap code. No hackery on this landing. Denied. Brick it all.

Let that little girl go, whiplash sharp for the Party and Princelings. For the Planet! Dammit.

Run faster, jump higher. Heroes bring joy. Protection is calm. The immense toil wrapped in … Shining Paths. Wilbur was suddenly flapping his steady arms at Kitty Hawk, like birds. Calm is perfection.

Crap, this is almost over. They're initiating landing sequences. What did Buck and Yuri do before stasis? Ivan *kildalled* the medical log? WTF!?

Bubbles, deploying. Not now … the fate of the Universal Principle is going to be decided during the commercial break!?

They raped her … twins.

She thinks I'm godlike, communicating. No physical presence, subconscious moral virtue piped in. A miracle. Ugh, never has a last gasp been so misunderstood. Can't even scream my lungs out.

Stay put Wil.e., Buck and Yuri are beating the doors, hands bloody. Suffocating. Fine. Last joke, blokes.

Li Peng is desperate, but out.

She hears the little quiet Jewish doctor, whispering to the little four year old girl wrapped in wet towels, stricken with diphtheria, "Sie wird leben."

She will live long enough too.

Stars. Water. Breathing. All of us?

Please … we need this.

National pride theories abound concerning the presumed failure of the first "manned" Mars mission. Li escaped a defective stasis pod. A shocked world audience saw an implacable Chinese star super nova. She planted an improvised depiction of the mythical Fenghuang in her dying moment.

The Campus Martius Mission was not considered a success by its nefarious backers.

Humanity rallied around the rescue of the two twins dubbed Remus and Romulus by the New Peng Convention. The little med-robot, designed by Honda, with retail med-AI, kept the boys alive until an eclectic team of Tibetan monks, Native American shaman and Catholic missionaries arrived. Subsequent missions included The New Porpoise Awareness Team.

To date, no State has been formed on the distant Red Planet. If one surfs upon the right brain waves, a Giant Serpent can still be felt below, wrapped around our little Blue Ball, hurdling through infinity.

ABOUT THE AUTHOR

Eric Sundwall almost made it to age fifty without writing a book. Having done so, he wonders if anyone will come knocking on his big red shed door.

www.ingramcontent.com/pod-product-compliance
Lightning Source LLC
Chambersburg PA
CBHW060551030426
42337CB00019B/3514